DATE DUE			
APR 2 4 2003			
DEC 1 9 2005			
MAR 9 2006			
		OCT 17 2006	

97067
796.357   Pietrusza, David.
Pie
          The Los Angeles
          Dodgers baseball
          team

ELEMENTARY SCHOOL DISTRICT #91
LOCKPORT, IL

440978 01842   46112A   002

★ GREAT SPORTS TEAMS ★

THE LOS ANGELES

BASEBALL TEAM

David Pietrusza

KELVIN GROVE SCHOOL
8th & Adams Street
Lockport, Illinois

Enslow Publishers, Inc.
44 Fadem Road   PO Box 38
Box 699   Aldershot
Springfield, NJ 07081   Hants GU12 6BP
USA   UK
http://www.enslow.com

Copyright © 1999 by Enslow Publishers, Inc.

All rights reserved.

No part of this book may be reproduced by any means without the written permission of the publisher.

Library of Congress Cataloging-in-Publication Data

Pietrusza, David, 1949–
    The Los Angeles Dodgers baseball team / David Pietrusza.
       p. cm. — (Great sports teams)
    Includes bibliographical references (p. 43) and index.
    Summary: A history of the baseball team that began in Brooklyn and moved to Los Angeles, focusing on its greatest players, managers, and seasons.
    ISBN 0-7660-1097-X
    1. Los Angeles Dodgers (Baseball team)—History—Juvenile literature.
[1. Los Angeles Dodgers (Baseball team)—History. 2. Baseball—History.]
I. Title. II. Series.
GV875.L6P52 1999
796.357′64′0979494—dc21   98-25726
                                                                    CIP
                                                                    AC

Printed in the United States of America

10 9 8 7 6 5 4 3 2 1

To Our Readers:
All Internet addresses in this book were active and appropriate when we went to press. Any comments or suggestions can be sent by e-mail to Comments@enslow.com or to the address on the back cover.

Illustration Credits: AP/Wide World Photos

Cover Illustration: AP/Wide World Photos

CONTENTS

1 Limping Hero 5

2 Pride of Brooklyn 11

3 Dodgers Immortals 17

4 Memorable Managers 23

5 Pitching and Speed 29

6 Decade of Change 35

Statistics 40

Chapter Notes 43

Glossary 44

Further Reading 46

Index 47

Where to Write 48

Tim Belcher played a large part in the success of the 1988 Dodgers. He started Game 1 of the World Series against the Oakland Athletics.

LIMPING HERO

The 1988 Los Angeles Dodgers were not the greatest team in baseball history; far from it. During the regular season, the New York Mets, champions of the National League's Eastern Division, had posted a much better record. In the rival American League, manager Tony LaRussa's Oakland A's featured sluggers Mark McGwire and league MVP Jose Canseco. Many considered the 1988 A's to be the beginning of a baseball dynasty.

Comeback Kids

But manager Tommy Lasorda's Dodgers had fought back all year. When the 1988 regular season ended, Los Angeles won the NL West over manager Pete Rose's Cincinnati Reds. In the National League Championship Series (NLCS), the Dodgers nipped the favored Mets in seven games. Now they faced the A's in the World Series. Their chances were not good. The

Orel Hershiser won both Game 2 and Game 5 of the 1988 World Series. He was named series MVP.

A's had won 104 games in the regular season, the Dodgers just 94.

The World Series opened at Los Angeles's Dodger Stadium. Helped by outfielder Mickey Hatcher's two-run homer, the Dodgers jumped to a 2–0 lead in the bottom of the first. The A's roared back in the top of second. Jose Canseco delivered a grand slam off Dodgers starter Tim Belcher, and suddenly the A's led 4–2. Los Angeles scored a run in the sixth to close the gap to 4–3. LaRussa brought in his relief ace, right-hander Dennis Eckersley, to pitch the ninth. Things looked extremely bad for the Dodgers.

Bench Strength

Eckersley got the first batter, catcher Mike Scioscia, to pop up. Then he struck out third baseman Jeff Hamilton. Now the Dodgers were down to their final out. Tommy Lasorda was thinking about calling on slugging outfielder Kirk Gibson to pinch hit for light-hitting shortstop Alfredo Griffin. Gibson led the Dodgers in homers during the regular season, but during the playoffs against the Mets, he pulled his left hamstring muscle while stealing second base. Worse than that, Gibson also had sprained the ligaments in his right knee. Only cortisone shots enabled the outfielder to get through the rest of the playoffs, and he did not start Game 1 of the World Series.

Gibson had not even been in the dugout during the game. Instead, deep in pain, he sat in the trainer's room. "I heard [NBC broadcaster] Vin Scully say they were looking for me on the bench," Gibson recalled,

Kirk Gibson came off the bench, barely able to stand, and hit a game-winning home run in the first game of the 1988 World Series.

"but that I probably wouldn't be able to play. I said, 'That's enough' and sent a batboy to get Tommy. I told him to go ahead and pinch hit for Alfredo and if he gets on, I'll give it my best shot."[1]

Lasorda sent up Mike Davis to pinch hit for Griffin. Davis walked, putting the tying run at first. Now Gibson got the call from Lasorda, and he hobbled into the dugout and grabbed a bat. He could barely walk up the steps onto the field and to home plate. The Dodger Stadium crowd went wild, but realistically it had to know the home team's chances were still slim. Even if Gibson got a safe hit to keep the rally alive, how could he run down to first?

Full Count

Eckersley got two quick strikes on Gibson. Then Gibson worked the count full. Eck threw a curveball. Gibson swung, and the ball took off like a rocket for the right-field stands—a two-run homer. Gibson gimped around the bases with the winning run, joyfully pumping his fist in the air. It was one of the greatest, most dramatic moments in World Series history.

Because Kirk Gibson's injury was so severe, he was unable to make another appearance in the 1988 Fall Classic. However, his ninth-inning, two-out heroics inspired his team to ultimately triumph over the favored Athletics. The Los Angeles Dodgers would become world champions.

Babe Herman (right) was one of the best hitters in baseball during the 1930s. Here he is talking with a Dodgers star of the 1970s, first baseman Steve Garvey.

PRIDE OF BROOKLYN

The Dodgers date back to 1884, when they entered the majors as part of the old American Association. They were based in Brooklyn then—back when Brooklyn was a separate city and not part of the City of New York. And back then, the Dodgers were known as the Bridegrooms—because so many of their players had just gotten married.

Early Days

The team switched leagues, to the National League in 1890, and became the Trolley Dodgers shortly afterward and the Superbas a little while after that. By the time the twentieth century rolled around, they were the Dodgers, but they were rarely very good. In the 1930s, one of the few stars Brooklyn boasted was outfielder Babe Herman. Herman could hit but couldn't field—he was once hit in the head with a foul ball. Another time he refused to slide into second base—he was afraid he would break the cigars he had in his back pocket.

True, the club won pennants in 1916 and 1920, but for the rest of the 1920s and 1930s, Brooklyn was usually a truly awful franchise—remembered as the Bums and the Daffiness Boys. That image began changing in 1938 with the arrival of Larry MacPhail as general manager. MacPhail was always thinking up new ways to do things. Earlier, when he ran the Cincinnati Reds, he had introduced night baseball to the major leagues. When MacPhail moved over to Brooklyn, he installed lights in the Dodgers' ballpark, Ebbets Field—and in 1939 he okayed the first television baseball broadcast ever. Scouting and trading for talented players, he turned the Dodgers from lovable, laughable losers into consistent winners.

Winning Ways

The Dodgers won the 1941 pennant, and starting in 1947 they captured pennant after pennant (although in 1951 their late-season collapse was among the most dramatic in sports history), bringing cheer to rabidly loyal Brooklyn fans. In the early 1950s, the powerful Dodgers were clearly the National League's greatest team, winning their first world championship in 1955.

A big part of being a Brooklyn Dodgers fan was going to Ebbets Field. Ebbets Field was a very cozy ballpark—just 31,497 seats. Brooklyn fans were famous for their loyalty, their knowledge of the game, and their enthusiasm. One group of Dodgers fans formed a five-man band, called the Dodger Sym-phony,

Dodgers fans in Brooklyn would flock to Ebbets Field to see their "Bums" play. Although the ballpark was torn down after the team left in 1957, the site of the old park is still a landmark.

to root for their team. They couldn't read music, but they played their hearts out for their team.

The Dodgers won pennants in 1947, 1949, 1952, and 1953—but the team still had its share of heartaches. The Dodgers lost the 1950 pennant on the last day of the season. In 1951, Brooklyn blew a 13 1/2 game lead over the arch rival New York Giants and were forced into a playoff with them for the National League pennant. The Bums were two runs ahead and just two outs away from the NL championship when the Giants' Bobby Thomson slammed a three-run

Pride of Brooklyn

*T*he Brooklyn Dodgers finally won a world title in 1955. Johnny Podres pitched the final out of Game 7, as the Dodgers beat the Yankees and became champions.

homer off Brooklyn relief pitcher Ralph Branca. "The Giants win the pennant, the Giants win the pennant!" shouted shocked but happy Giants announcer Russ Hodges.[1] Dodger fans were just as shocked—but they weren't happy.

Finally, in 1955, Brooklyn had its dream come true. Its once downtrodden team beat the mighty New York Yankees in the World Series. The Dodgers were now champions of the world! "Everyone in the Dodgers organization was thrilled beyond comprehension," recalled manager Walter Alston. "It was a great win. A great hour for a bunch of guys who had an unbelievable year."[2]

Going Out West

The Dodgers won another pennant in 1956, but suddenly the bubble burst. Dodgers owner Walter O'Malley moved the franchise to Los Angeles after the 1957 season. He is still hated in Brooklyn for that, but the move helped make baseball a truly national sport.

A new Dodgers era was about to begin.

Hall of Famer Jackie Robinson (42), the first African American to play in the major leagues, played an exciting style of baseball. Here he is stealing home in the 1955 World Series.

DODGERS IMMORTALS

The Dodgers could not have won so many pennants without featuring some of the greatest stars in the game's history.

Pee Wee Reese

When the Dodgers once again became a winning team in 1941, a key player was shortstop Harold "Pee Wee" Reese. Despite his nickname, Pee Wee was not particularly short; as a boy he had often shot marbles, and he had been named for a marble called a Pee Wee. The solid-fielding Reese solidified the formerly shaky Dodgers infield, hit very well for a shortstop, and provided leadership both on and off the field. Reese, the Dodgers' team captain, helped more than any other player to transform Brooklyn's Bums into champions. He was elected to the Baseball Hall of Fame in 1984.

Jackie Robinson

Until 1947, modern baseball had not allowed either American-born or Caribbean blacks to play. All that changed when Brooklyn general manager Branch Rickey brought up an exciting Negro League infielder named Jackie Robinson. Robinson faced a tremendous challenge. Some of his teammates did not want to play with him (Pee Wee Reese was not among them; he welcomed Robinson to the team). Rival players and fans flung racial insults at Robinson. He received numerous death threats. In spring training in the segregated South, he often could not stay in hotels with his white teammates. Yet Robinson overcame all of that. His aggressive style of baserunning helped unnerve opponents and transform the Dodgers from merely a very good team into a *great* team. "He is the only player I ever saw," slugging Pittsburgh outfielder Ralph Kiner once recalled, "who could turn a game around completely by himself."[1]

In 1947, Robinson won Rookie of the Year honors. In 1949, he was named National League Most Valuable Player (MVP). In 1962, he became the first African American ever elected to the Baseball Hall of Fame.

Roy Campanella

Brooklyn catcher Roy Campanella was also among the first African Americans to integrate the game. Unlike Robinson, who was a very serious and intense competitor, Campanella was an extremely cheerful and popular individual. He was also one of the

Roy Campanella won 3 MVP Awards as a member of the Brooklyn Dodgers. Here, Campanella is swinging for the fences.

greatest catchers of all-time, and he won National League MVP honors in 1951, 1953, and 1955.

In January 1958, Campy's career came to a tragic end. While he was driving home from his business, Campanella's car skidded into a telephone pole. The accident left him paralyzed in both his arms and legs. On Campy's birthday (May 7) in 1959, the biggest crowd in big-league history turned out to honor the beloved catcher. After he spoke, the stadium lights were turned off, and every one of the 93,103 fans there lit a match in Campy's honor. "It was a gesture," he commented, "for my benefit, in the form of a huge birthday cake. I've never seen anything like it."[2] Campanella was inducted into the Hall of Fame in 1969.

Both Sandy Koufax (front) and Don Drysdale (back) were hard throwing pitchers. With them on the staff, the Dodgers won three world titles from 1959–65.

Sandy Koufax and Don Drysdale

In the 1960s, the Dodgers (by then in Los Angeles) featured two overpowering pitchers, Sandy Koufax and Don Drysdale. The right-handed Drysdale was known for his intimidating style of pitching. Dig in against Big D—as he was often called—and he would dust you back with a pitch. He also would not hesitate to throw at enemy batters if an opposing pitcher had thrown at a Dodgers batter. "When I was on the mound," Drysdale boasted, "the Dodgers knew they were going to be protected."[3]

Brooklyn-born Sandy Koufax could throw even harder than Drysdale, but he was a much quieter—even a shy—individual. When Koufax first joined the Dodgers, he was extremely wild and not very effective. Once he learned to get his pitches into the strike zone, however, he was nearly unbeatable. From 1962 through 1966, Koufax led the NL in ERA 5 times, was 111–34, and threw 4 no-hitters, including a perfect game against the Cubs in 1965.

Both Koufax and Drysdale had to be excellent pitchers to compile winning records with the weak-hitting Dodger offense behind them. Once Drysdale was told that Koufax had pitched a no-hitter. "Did he win?" Drysdale wanted to know.[4]

On to Cooperstown

Koufax's career ended very quickly. He was just thirty years old and the most dominating pitcher in baseball, when arthritis in his pitching arm ended his career. "I don't regret one minute of the last twelve years," a saddened Koufax quietly told reporters, "The only thing I regret is leaving baseball."[5] Sandy Koufax entered the Hall of Fame in his first year of eligibility, in 1972. Don Drysdale had to wait. He entered Cooperstown in 1984.

Wilbert "Uncle Robbie" Robinson lead the Dodgers to 2 pennants. He was inducted into the Hall of Fame in 1945.

MEMORABLE MANAGERS

The Dodgers have been led by several of baseball's most famous managers—Wilbert "Uncle Robbie" Robinson, Leo "The Lip" Durocher, Walter "Smoky" Alston, and Tommy Lasorda. All are members of the Baseball Hall of Fame.

Uncle Robbie

Wilbert Robinson was so popular in Brooklyn that the Dodgers were renamed the Robins in his honor. He led the franchise to pennants in 1916 and 1920, but he is best remembered for the many terrible Brooklyn teams he later managed. These clubs were known as the Daffiness Boys. Uncle Robbie's players caroused at night, missed coaches' signs, and read newspapers in the dugout. Robinson tried cracking down by instituting a Bonehead Club. Anyone who committed a "bonehead" play would be fined. However, when Uncle Robbie delivered a laundry list—instead of the

Brooklyn lineup card—to the home-plate umpire, he became the Bonehead Club's first member. Embarrassed by his mistake, he quickly abandoned the idea of the club.

Leo "The Lip" Durocher

Leo Durocher took charge of the Dodgers in 1939. By 1941, this tough former infielder had led the Dodgers to their first pennant since 1920. The Lip would do anything to win. His style bothered many. He was brash, boastful, and often associated with known gamblers. "Nice guys finish last" was supposed to be his motto.[1] Baseball Commissioner Happy Chandler tired of tolerating Durocher's gambling habits and banned him from the game for the entire 1947 season. The Dodgers won the pennant without him.

Walter Alston

In 1953, Brooklyn manager Charlie Dressen won the pennant for the second year in a row and demanded a two-year contract. Owner Walter O'Malley fired Dressen and appointed Walter Alston as his replacement. Alston, a veteran minor-league manager (who had enjoyed only one at bat—and struck out—as a major-league player) lasted twenty-three seasons on one-year contracts. Smoky Alston was low-key and conservative as a manager. Some even called him colorless. But he won world championships in 1955 and 1959 (and a pennant in 1956), led his team to a tie for the flag in 1962 before losing a playoff to the San Francisco Giants, and won world championships

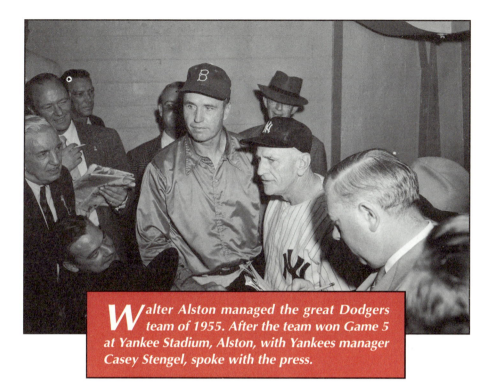

*W*alter Alston managed the great Dodgers team of 1955. After the team won Game 5 at Yankee Stadium, Alston, with Yankees manager Casey Stengel, spoke with the press.

again in 1963 and 1965 and pennants in 1966 and 1974. He was named Manager of the Year three times by *The Sporting News*, five times by United Press International, and six times by the Associated Press. Walter Alston finally retired in September 1976. He had managed the Dodgers longer than anyone else had ever managed a single team—with the exception of legendary managers Connie Mack of the A's and John McGraw of the Giants.

Tommy Lasorda

The man who replaced Walter Alston was the jovial and outgoing Tommy Lasorda. He loved to socialize

*T*ommy Lasorda leads the charge out of the Dodgers dugout after his team recorded the final out of the 1981 World Series.

with his players and was noted for his cheerfulness and his unusual loyalty to the Dodgers organization. "I bleed Dodger blue," he would tell anyone who would listen, "and when I die, I'm going to the Big Dodger in the Sky."[2] Some thought Lasorda was just a clown. "Tommy's amazing," said pitcher Don Sutton. "Why, he'll even talk to numbers on an elevator. When they're lit up, he thinks they're listening."[3] But his unusual style paid off. He won four pennants and two world championships and usually brought the Dodgers home as winners each year. Lasorda also served as the Dodgers interim general manager in 1998.

Branch Rickey

Another member of Dodgers management has already been enshrined in the Hall of Fame—but he was not a field manager. He was General Manager Branch Rickey. Before coming to the Dodgers, Rickey had been with the Cardinals. While he was there, he had developed the farm-system concept, revolutionizing baseball. With the Dodgers, Rickey decided to do something even more revolutionary: end baseball's color line. In December 1945, he signed Negro League infielder Jackie Robinson to a Dodgers minor-league contract. "I don't mean to be a crusader," Rickey explained. "My only purpose is to be fair to all people and my selfish objective is to win baseball games."[4] With Jackie Robinson, the Dodgers would not only win ball games—they would win six pennants in ten years. And they would change not only the face of baseball but the face of America itself.

Memorable Managers

Beating the throw from the outfield, Maury Wills slides safely into third base. Wills was a threat to steal every time he reached base.

PITCHING AND SPEED

The Dodgers' first California home was a temporary one, the huge Los Angeles Coliseum—a 93,600 seat stadium. The Coliseum was built for Olympic events and featured weird dimensions for baseball. Though the building itself was huge, it was just 251 feet down the left-field line. The Dodgers were not an immediate success in this cavernous new home. They sunk to seventh place in 1958 but rebounded in 1959 to win their second world championship. When their permanent ballpark, beautiful fifty-six thousand seat Dodger Stadium, was completed in 1962, the ballclub was happy to move into it.

1960s

In the 1960s, the Dodgers under manager Walter Alston were a highly successful team that relied on strong pitching and speed. The pitching staff was led by left-hander Sandy Koufax and right-hander Don

Drysdale. The lineup included two of the league's top base thieves, shortstop Maury Wills and center fielder Willie Davis. In 1962, Wills broke Hall of Famer Ty Cobb's season record of 96 stolen bases by swiping 104. "My instructions for preventing Wills from stealing are simple," said Cincinnati Reds manager Fred Hutchinson. "Don't let him get on base."[1] Wills's daring baserunning helped make the stolen base an important part of modern baseball offensive strategy.

The Los Angeles Dodgers' biggest disappointment came in 1962. The team was in first place for most of the season. With four games left, they needed to win only one game to clinch the championship. Instead, they dropped all four contests and were forced into a three-game playoff against their hated rivals, the Giants, now playing in San Francisco. In Game 3, the Dodgers led, 4–2, going into the ninth inning but lost yet another heartbreaker to the Giants.

Champs

The Dodgers, however, bounced back to win world championships in 1963 (defeating the Yankees in the Series) and 1965 (defeating the Minnesota Twins) and the National League pennant in 1966. Sandy Koufax, suffering from elbow problems, retired after the 1966 season. Don Drysdale continued to pitch for the Dodgers. In 1968 he set a major-league record (since broken by Dodger Orel Hershiser) by hurling 58 consecutive scoreless innings. Drysdale also pitched a record six straight shutouts.

Into the windup, Sandy Koufax looks to blow the ball past the opposing batter. On September 9, 1965, Koufax threw a perfect game.

1974-78

The Dodgers, however, did not capture another National League pennant until 1974 when Los Angeles relief pitcher Mike Marshall set a major-league record with 106 appearances and won the NL Cy Young Award. The Dodgers lost the World Series in five games that year to Oakland. In 1977 and 1978, they won pennants—but each time lost the Series in six games to the New York Yankees. They were still very popular with the fans, however. In 1978, the Dodgers became the first team to draw 3 million fans.

1981

In 1981, the Dodgers finally won another world championship behind their longtime infield of first

In 1981, Fernando Valenzuela took the baseball world by storm. That year he won both the National League Rookie of the Year and Cy Young Awards.

baseman Steve Garvey, second baseman Davey Lopes, shortstop Bill Russell, and third baseman Ron "The Penguin" Cey. Mexican pitching sensation Fernando Valenzuela won both the Rookie of the Year and the Cy Young Awards. Valenzuela was absolutely devastating when he first reached the majors. The southpaw did not allow an earned run in the first 17 2/3 innings he pitched for the Dodgers. He had been equally effective in the minors—combining that total with his unscored streak at the Dodgers' San Antonio farm club, he had a string of 52 2/3 straight scoreless innings. He also won his first ten major-league decisions.

In 1981's World Series, the Dodgers avenged their 1977 and 1978 Series losses to George Steinbrenner's Yankees, defeating the Bronx Bombers in six games as Garvey batted .417 and outfielder Pedro Guerrero drove in seven runs.

1988

The pennant-winning 1988 Dodgers featured pitchers Orel Hershiser (23–8) and Tim Leary (17–11), and outfielders Kirk Gibson (25 homers) and Mike Marshall (20 homers). In that fall's World Series, Los Angeles stunned the favored Oakland A's, winning in just five games. They were helped not only by Gibson's dramatic Game 1 homer, but also by Hershiser's two wins.

Decade after decade, in their California home, the Dodgers have built a winning tradition.

When Mike Piazza finished playing college baseball not many people thought he was a pro prospect. Surprisingly, he has developed into one of the greatest hitting catchers of all-time.

DECADE OF CHANGE

In 1988, not only did Kirk Gibson and the Dodgers capture the World Championship; Los Angeles pitcher Orel Hershiser broke a record many thought would last forever. Back in 1968, Don Drysdale had recorded 58 consecutive scoreless innings. Late in 1988, Hershiser threw 59 straight scoreless innings, ending with 10 shutout innings against the Padres on September 28, 1988.

Young Guns

In 1992, starting with first baseman Eric Karros, the Dodgers began a string of winning five straight National League Rookie of the Year awards. The next season, hard-hitting catcher Mike Piazza drove in 112 runs to become the unanimous winner. But when Mike Piazza graduated from Miami-Dade County Community College in 1988, no major-league team wanted to draft him. Only because Piazza's father was friends with Dodgers manager Tommy Lasorda did Los Angeles draft Piazza. Even then, they only took him in the 62nd round. Of the 1,433 players selected in that year's free agent draft, he was number 1,390. "Everything this kid is," Lasorda once said, "he made himself. When I judge players, friendship has nothing to do with it."[1]

In 1994, Dodgers right fielder Raul Mondesi captured Rookie honors. Not only does Mondesi hit for average and power; he boasts one of the finest throwing arms among major-league outfielders.

The Finest Imports

The Dodgers led the NL West as the player's strike ended the 1994 season; in 1995, they posted a 78–66 (.542) record, to capture the National League's Western Division for the first time since their World Championship year of 1988. The pitching both of Ramon Martinez and of rookie Hideo Nomo helped the team to finish first. Martinez no-hit the Florida Marlins on July 14, 1995. Nomo was a superstar in his native Japan before joining the Dodgers. He led the Japanese Pacific League in wins and strikeouts each season from 1990 through 1993, and he paced the JPL with a 2.91 ERA in 1990. In 1995, he captured NL Rookie of the Year honors.

Yet in the postseason, Dodgers pitching was nothing to brag about. In the division series, the team's staff posted a horrible 6.92 ERA, and the Cincinnati Reds swept Los Angeles in three straight games.

Hideo Nomo came to the Dodgers after a stellar career in Japan. In 1995, he won the NL Rookie of the Year Award.

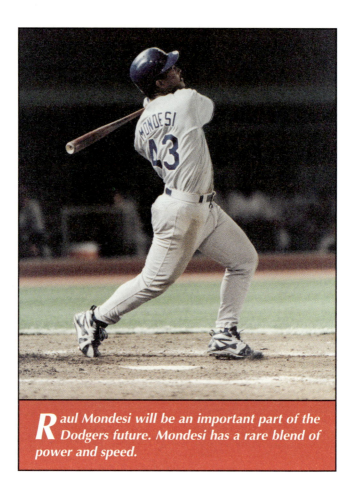

Raul Mondesi will be an important part of the Dodgers future. Mondesi has a rare blend of power and speed.

Playoff Contenders

The 1996 Dodgers battled some severe health problems but still entered postseason play. In July 1996, shortly after Tommy Lasorda underwent heart surgery, he announced his retirement as Dodgers manager. Dodgers coach Bill Russell replaced Lasorda at the helm. Meanwhile, cancer struck Los Angeles center fielder Brett Butler. After surgery and chemotherapy, Butler bravely returned to action in

August. Sadly, just a few days later, he was hit on the hand with a pitch and again entered the disabled list.

Under Bill Russell the Dodgers finished 1996 with a 90–72 (.555) record and won the NL wild card berth. Helping the team to the postseason were a number of individual accomplishments. Hideo Nomo became the twentieth Dodger to pitch a no-hitter when he threw one at Denver's hitter-friendly Coors Field on September 17, 1996. Mike Piazza set a new Los Angeles (but not Dodgers) record with 36 homers. And outfielder Todd Hollandsworth became the fifth consecutive Dodger to win National League rookie honors.

Unfortunately, in the postseason, the Dodgers' bats were cold. Los Angeles hitters batted a mere .147 against the mighty Atlanta pitching staff and were again swept in the first playoff round in three straight.

Changing Times

In 1998, much changed. Nomo and Piazza were traded. Manager Bill Russell was fired. He was replaced by Glenn Hoffman, then Davey Johnson. No longer would the O'Malley family own the team. For an estimated $350 million, Peter O'Malley had sold the Dodgers to the Fox Group, owned by media mogul Rupert Murdoch. "I believe Fox Group will be an outstanding owner of the Dodgers,"[2] said Peter O'Malley of the company that owned the Fox Television Network as well as numerous newspapers and broadcasting operations. Whoever owns the Dodgers, though, they will continue to be one of America's great sports teams.

STATISTICS

Team Record

The Dodgers History

YEARS	LOCATION	W	L	PCT.	PENNANTS	WORLD SERIES
1884–89*	Brooklyn	410	354	.537	1889	None
1890–99**	Brooklyn	722	644	.529	1890***	None
1900–09	Brooklyn	649	809	.445	1900***	None
1910–19	Brooklyn	696	787	.469	1916	None
1920–29	Brooklyn	765	768	.499	1920	None
1930–39	Brooklyn	734	793	.481	None	None
1940–49	Brooklyn	894	646	.581	1941, 1947, 1949	None
1950–59‡	Brooklyn Los Angeles	913	630	.592	1952–53, 1955–56, 1959	1955, 1959
1960–69	Los Angeles	878	729	.546	1963, 1965–66	1963, 1965
1970–79	Los Angeles	910	701	.565	1974, 1977–78	None
1980–89	Los Angeles	825	741	.527	1981, 1988	1981, 1988
1990–98	Los Angeles	720	672	.517	None	None

The Dodgers Today

YEAR	W	L	PCT.	COACH	DIVISION FINISH
1990	86	76	.531	Tommy Lasorda	2nd
1991	93	69	.574	Tommy Lasorda	2nd
1992	63	99	.389	Tommy Lasorda	6th

The Los Angeles Dodgers Baseball Team

The Dodgers Today (con't)

YEAR	W	L	PCT.	COACH	DIVISION FINISH
1993	81	81	.500	Tommy Lasorda	4th
1994	58	56	.509	Tommy Lasorda	1st
1995	78	66	.542	Tommy Lasorda	1st
1996	90	72	.556	Tommy Lasorda Bill Russell	2nd
1997	88	74	.543	Bill Russell	2nd
1998	83	79	.512	Bill Russell Glenn Hoffman	3rd

Total History

W	L	PCT.	PENNANTS	WORLD SERIES
9,116	8,274	.524	21	6

W=Wins
L=Losses
PCT.=Winning Percentage
PENNANTS=Won league title
WORLD SERIES=Won World Series

*Played in the American Association.
**Joined the National League prior to the 1890 season.
***Won NL championship, World Series did not exist until 1903.
‡Moved to Los Angeles prior to the 1958 season.

Championship Managers

MANAGER	YEARS MANAGED	RECORD	WORLD CHAMPIONSHIPS
Bill McGunnigle	1888–90	267–139	1890
Ned Hanlon	1899–1905	511–488	1900
Walter Alston	1954–76	2,040–1,613	1955, 1959, 1963, 1965
Tommy Lasorda	1976–96	1,599–1,439	1981, 1988

Statistics

Great Hitters

	CAREER STATISTICS									
PLAYER	SEA	YRS	G	AB	R	H	HR	RBI	SB	AVG
Roy Campanella*	1948–57	10	1,215	4,205	627	1,161	242	856	25	.276
Steve Garvey	1969–82	19	2,332	8,835	1,143	2,599	272	1,308	83	.294
Kirk Gibson	1988–90	17	1,635	5,798	985	1,553	255	870	284	.268
Gil Hodges	1943, 1947–61	18	2,071	7,030	1,105	1,921	370	1,274	63	.273
Raul Mondesi	1993–	6	757	2,886	445	852	130	419	104	.295
Mike Piazza	1992–98	7	840	3,119	511	1,038	200	644	11	.333
Pee Wee Reese*	1940–42 1946–58	16	2,166	8,058	1,338	2,170	126	885	232	.269
Jackie Robinson*	1947–56	10	1,382	4,877	947	1,518	137	734	197	.311
Duke Snider*	1947–62	18	2,143	7,161	1,259	2,116	407	1,333	99	.295
Zack Wheat*	1909–26	19	2,410	9,106	1,289	2,884	132	1,248	205	.317

SEA=Seasons with Dodgers
YRS=Years in the Majors
G=Games
AB=At Bats
R=Runs Scored
H=Hits
HR=Home Runs
RBI=Runs Batted In
SB=Stolen Bases
AVG=Batting Average

Great Pitchers

	CAREER STATISTICS									
PLAYER	SEA	YRS	W	L	PCT	ERA	G	SV	IP	K	SH
Don Drysdale*	1956–69	14	209	166	.557	2.95	518	6	3,432	2,486	49
Orel Hershiser	1983–94	16	190	133	.588	3.33	468	5	2,927	1,912	25
Sandy Koufax*	1955–66	12	165	87	.655	2.76	397	9	2,324	2,396	40
Ramon Martinez	1988–98	11	123	77	.615	3.45	266	0	1,732	1,314	20
Don Sutton*	1966–80 1988	23	324	256	.559	3.26	774	5	5,282	3,574	58

SEA=Seasons with Dodgers
YRS=Years in the Majors
W=Wins
L=Losses
PCT=Winning Percentage
ERA=Earned Run Average
G=Games
SV=Saves
IP=Innings Pitched
K=Strikeouts
SH=Shutouts

*Hall of Fame members

CHAPTER NOTES

Chapter 1: Limping Hero
1. *The Sporting News Baseball Guide: 1989 Edition* (St. Louis: The Sporting News Publishing Company, 1989), p. 217.

Chapter 2: Pride of Brooklyn
1. Stanley Cohen, *Dodgers!: The First 100 Years* (New York: Birch Lane Press, 1990), p. 102.

2. Dan Riley, ed., *The Dodgers Reader* (Boston: Houghton Mifflin, 1992), p. 122.

Chapter 3: Dodgers Immortals
1. Peter C. Bjarkman, *Top 10 Baseball Base Stealers* (Springfield, N.J.: Enslow Publishers, Inc., 1995), p. 40.

2. Roy Campanella, *It's Good to Be Alive* (Boston: Little, Brown, and Co., 1959), p. 228.

3. Don Drysdale (with Bob Verdi), *Once a Bum Always a Dodger* (New York: St. Martin's Press, 1990), p. 185.

4. Stanley Cohen, *Dodgers!: The First 100 Years* (New York: Birch Lane Press, 1990), p. 152.

5. George Vecsey, *The Baseball Life of Sandy Koufax* (New York: Scholastic Book Service, 1968), p. 211.

Chapter 4: Memorable Managers
1. Hank Nuwar, *Strategies of the Great Baseball Managers* (New York: Franklin Watts, 1988), pp. 102–103.

2. Paul Dickson, *Baseball's Greatest Quotations* (New York: HarperCollins, 1991), p. 240.

3. Bill Adler, *Baseball Wit* (New York: Crown, 1986), p. 100.

4. Jules Tygiel, *Baseball's Great Experiment* (New York: Oxford, 1983), p. 52.

Chapter 5: Pitching and Speed
1. Kevin Nelson, *Baseball's Greatest Quotes* (New York: Simon & Schuster, 1982), p. 105.

Chapter 6: Decade of Change
1. Mel Antonen, "Piazza Works Hard on Fundamentals," *USA Today*, October 28, 1993, p. 3C.

2. Paul Fahri, "Dodgers, Murdoch Reach Agreement," *Washington Post*, September 5, 1997.

GLOSSARY

American Association—A defunct major league that operated from 1882 through 1991. Not to be confused with a minor league by the same name.

American League—One of the two current major leagues of baseball, founded in 1901 by Ban Johnson. The other major league is the National League. The primary difference between the two leagues is that since 1973 the American League (AL) has used the designated hitter rule.

batting average—The number of hits divided by the number of at bats.

commissioner—Baseball's highest official; the office was established in 1920 and first filled by Judge Kenesaw Mountain Landis.

Cy Young Award—An award given each year to the best pitcher in each major league.

designated hitter—A player who does not take the field during the game, but only bats. In the major leagues, the designated hitter (DH) is used only in American League ballparks.

ERA (Earned Run Average)—The number of earned runs divided by the number of innings pitched times nine; the ERA is perhaps the best measure of pitching effectiveness.

farm system—The system in which major-league baseball clubs develop talent through a network of minor-league clubs. The major-league clubs fund the minor-league clubs; in return, the minor-league clubs send players to their parent major-league clubs.

fly ball—A ball hit in the air, as opposed to a ground ball.

free agent—A major leaguer whose contractual obligations to his old team have expired and who is free to sign with any major-league team.

general manager—The official in charge of a ballclub's business and personnel matters.

Gold Glove Award—An award given annually to the best fielder at each position in both the National and American Leagues.

Hall of Fame—Located in Cooperstown, New York. Membership in the National Baseball Hall of Fame is the highest honor that can be awarded to a professional player.

hold out—A player who, desiring additional salary, does not return his contract for the upcoming season.

homer—Home run.

infielder—One who plays an infield position (first base, second base, third base, or shortstop).

Japan Pacific League—One of the two Japanese major leagues.

League Championship Series (LCS)—The best-of-seven series that determines the American and National League champions.

National League—The oldest surviving major league, founded in 1876 by William Hulbert; sometimes called the "senior circuit."

Negro League—A baseball league in which African-American players performed before they were allowed into organized baseball.

pennant—A league championship, alternately called the flag.

perfect game—A game in which a pitcher retires all twenty-seven batters he faces.

pivot man—The relay player at second base during a double play.

platooning—Alternating players at a given position to take advantage of their strengths, usually taking into consideration whether they are left- or right-handed hitters.

southpaw—A left-hander.

stolen base—A play in which the base runner advances to another base while the pitcher takes his motion.

wildcard—The nondivision winning club with the best won-lost percentage in regular season play; the wildcard team in each league earns a berth in postseason play.

World Series—The end of the season best-of-seven series that pits the champions of the National and American leagues against each other.

Glossary

FURTHER READING

Adler, David A,. and Robert Casilla. *A Picture Book of Jackie Robinson*. New York: Holiday House, 1997.

Alvarez, Mark. *The Official Hall of Fame Story of Jackie Robinson*. New York: Little Simon, 1990.

Campanella, Roy. *It's Good to Be Alive*. Boston: Little, Brown and Co., 1959.

Chadwick, Bruce, and David M. Spindel. *The Dodgers: Memories and Memorabilia from Brooklyn to L.A.* New York: Abbeville, 1993.

Cohen, Stanley. *Dodgers!: The First 100 Years*. New York: Birch Lane, 1990.

Coombs, Karen Mueller. *Jackie Robinson: Baseball's Civil Rights Legend*. Springfield, N.J.: Enslow Publishers, 1997.

Golenbock, Peter, and Paul Bacon. *Teammates*. San Diego: Harcourt Brace, 1990.

Grabowski, John F. *Jackie Robinson*. New York: Chelsea House, 1990.

———. *Sandy Koufax*. New York: Chelsea House, 1992.

James, Brant. *Mike Piazza*. New York: Chelsea House, 1997.

Knapp, Ron. *Sports Great Orel Hershiser*. Springfield, N.J.: Enslow Publishers, 1993.

Lasorda, Tommy (with David Fisher). *The Artful Dodger*. New York: Arbor House, 1985.

Macht, Norman L. *Roy Campanella: Baseball Star*. New York: Chelsea House, 1996.

Nuwar, Hank. *Strategies of the Great Baseball Managers*. New York: Franklin Watts, 1988.

Pietrusza, David. *Top 10 Baseball Managers*. Springfield, N.J.: Enslow Publishers, 1999.

Rosenblum, Richard. *Brooklyn Dodger Days*. New York: Atheneum, 1991.

Vecsey, George. *The Baseball Life of Sandy Koufax*. New York: Scholastic Book Service, 1968.

Zimmerman, Tom. *A Day in the Season of the L.A. Dodgers*. New York: Shapolsky Books, 1990.

INDEX

A
Alston, Walter, 15, 23, 24–25, 29
American Association, 11
Atlanta Braves, 39

B
Belcher, Tim, 7
Branca, Ralph, 15
Brooklyn Bridegrooms, 11
Brooklyn Dodgers, 11–15, 17–19, 23, 24
Brooklyn Robins, 23
Brooklyn Superbas, 11
Brooklyn Trolley Dodgers, 11
Butler, Brett, 38–39

C
Campanella, Roy, 18–19
Canseco, Jose, 5, 7
Cey, Ron, 33
Chandler, Happy, 24
Chicago Cubs, 21
Cincinnati Reds, 5, 12, 30, 36
Cobb, Ty, 30
Coors Field, 39
Cy Young Award, 31, 33

D
Davis, Mike, 9
Davis, Willie, 30
Dodger Stadium, 7, 9, 29
Dressen, Charlie, 24
Drysdale, Don, 20–21, 29–30, 35
Durocher, Leo, 23, 24

E
Ebbets Field, 12
Eckersley, Dennis, 7, 9

F
Florida Marlins, 36

G
Garvey, Steve, 33

Gibson, Kirk, 7–9
Griffin, Alfredo, 7, 9
Guerrero, Pedro, 33

H
Hatcher, Mickey, 7
Hershiser, Orel, 30, 33, 35
Hodges, Russ, 15
Hollandsworth, Todd, 39
Hutchinson, Fred, 30

J
Japanese Pacific League, 36

K
Karros, Eric, 35
Kiner, Ralph, 18
Koufax, Sandy, 20–21, 29–30

L
LaRussa, Tony, 5, 7
Lasorda, Tommy, 5, 7, 23, 25–27, 36, 38
Leary, Tim, 33
Lopes, Davey, 33

M
Mack, Connie, 25
MacPhail, Larry, 12
Marshall, Mike (first baseman), 33
Marshall, Mike (pitcher), 31
Martinez, Ramon, 36
McGraw, John, 25
McGwire, Mark, 5
Minnesota Twins, 30
Mondesi, Raul, 36
Murdoch, Rupert, 39
MVP Award, 5, 18, 19

N
National Baseball Hall of Fame, 17, 18, 19, 21, 27, 30
National League Championship Series (1988), 5

Negro Leagues, 18, 27
New York Giants, 13, 25
New York Mets, 5, 7
New York Yankees, 15, 30, 31, 33
Nomo, Hideo, 36, 39

O
Oakland Athletics, 4, 5, 7, 9, 31, 33
O'Malley, Peter, 39
O'Malley, Walter, 15, 24

P
Piazza, Mike, 35–36, 39
Pittsburgh Pirates, 18

R
Reese, Pee Wee, 17, 18
Rickey, Branch, 18, 27
Robinson, Jackie, 18, 27
Robinson, Wilbert, 23–24
Rookie of the Year Award, 18, 33, 35, 36, 39
Rose, Pete, 5
Russell, Bill, 33, 38–39

S
St. Louis Cardinals, 27
San Diego Padres, 35
San Francisco Giants, 24, 30
Scioscia, Mike, 7
Scully, Vin, 7
Sporting News, The, 25
Steinbrenner, George, 33
Sutton, Don, 27

T
Thomson, Bobby, 13

W
Wills, Maury, 30
World Series (1955), 15
World Series (1974), 31
World Series (1977), 31, 33
World Series (1978), 31, 33
World Series (1981), 33
World Series (1988), 5–9, 33, 35, 36

WHERE TO WRITE

Los Angeles Dodgers
Dodger Stadium
1000 Elysian Park Avenue
Los Angeles, California
90012-1199

WEBSITE

http://www.dodgers.com
http://www.majorleaguebaseball.com/nl/la
http://www.totaldodgers.com